Finder's Keepers

Finder's... so you'll know where to find the recipes you want to try.

Keepers... so you won't let the best recipes get away.

Your Recipe Collection

L B Publications

Additional copies of **FINDER'S KEEPERS** may be ordered by sending $9.95 per book plus $2.00 for postage and handling. (Texas residents add $.80 sales tax.) Send check to the following address.

LB Publications
8338 San Leandro
Dallas, Texas 75218

Library of Congress Catalogue Card #
ISBN: 0-9616746-0-1
First Printing July 1986 5,000 copies
Second Printing April 1988 3,000 copies

Printed by
WIMMER BROTHERS
Memphis Dallas

Contents

Appetizers–Beverages Breads–Eggs

Favorite Recipe Index

Recipe Name	Pan Cinnamon Rolls - Dough best for caramel rolls	
Cookbook	The Stouffer Cookbook	Page 138
Recipe Name	Southern Orange Rolls	
Cookbook	The Stouffer Cookbook	Page 142
Recipe Name	Ring-a-Lings Good	
Cookbook	Pillsbury Bake Off Classics	Page 17
Recipe Name	Puff Pillow Buns (cream cheese filling	
Cookbook	Better Homes & Gardens Bread Cookbook	Page 26
Recipe Name		
Cookbook		Page
Recipe Name		
Cookbook		Page
Recipe Name		
Cookbook		Page
Recipe Name		
Cookbook		Page
Recipe Name		
Cookbook		Page
Recipe Name		
Cookbook		Page
Recipe Name		
Cookbook		Page

Favorite Recipe Index

Recipe Name	
Cookbook	Page
Recipe Name	
Cookbook	Page
Recipe Name	
Cookbook	Page
Recipe Name	
Cookbook	Page
Recipe Name	
Cookbook	Page
Recipe Name	
Cookbook	Page
Recipe Name	
Cookbook	Page
Recipe Name	
Cookbook	Page
Recipe Name	
Cookbook	Page
Recipe Name	
Cookbook	Page
Recipe Name	
Cookbook	Page

Favorite Recipe Index

Recipe Name	
Cookbook	Page
Recipe Name	
Cookbook	Page
Recipe Name	
Cookbook	Page
Recipe Name	
Cookbook	Page
Recipe Name	
Cookbook	Page
Recipe Name	
Cookbook	Page
Recipe Name	
Cookbook	Page
Recipe Name	
Cookbook	Page
Recipe Name	
Cookbook	Page
Recipe Name	
Cookbook	Page
Recipe Name	
Cookbook	Page

Favorite Recipe Index

Recipe Name	
Cookbook	Page
Recipe Name	
Cookbook	Page
Recipe Name	
Cookbook	Page
Recipe Name	
Cookbook	Page
Recipe Name	
Cookbook	Page
Recipe Name	
Cookbook	Page
Recipe Name	
Cookbook	Page
Recipe Name	
Cookbook	Page
Recipe Name	
Cookbook	Page
Recipe Name	
Cookbook	Page
Recipe Name	
Cookbook	Page

Favorite Recipes

Recipe Name	
From	Serves/ Yield

Favorite Recipes

Recipe Name	
From	Serves/ Yield

Favorite Recipes

Recipe Name	
From	Serves/ Yield

Favorite Recipes

Recipe Name	
From	Serves/ Yield

Favorite Recipes

Recipe Name	
From	Serves/ Yield

Favorite Recipes

Recipe Name	
From	Serves/ Yield

Favorite Recipes

Recipe Name	
From	Serves/ Yield

Favorite Recipes

Recipe Name	
From	Serves/ Yield

Favorite Recipes

Recipe Name	
From	Serves/ Yield

Favorite Recipes

Recipe Name	
From	Serves/ Yield

Favorite Recipes

Recipe Name	
From	Serves/ Yield

Favorite Recipes

Recipe Name	
From	Serves/ Yield

Favorite Recipes

Recipe Name	
From	Serves/ Yield

Favorite Recipes

Recipe Name	
From	Serves/ Yield

Favorite Recipes

Recipe Name	
From	Serves/ Yield

Favorite Recipes

Recipe Name	
From	Serves/ Yield

Salads–Dressings
Soups–Sandwiches

Favorite Recipe Index

Recipe Name	
Cookbook	Page
Recipe Name	
Cookbook	Page
Recipe Name	
Cookbook	Page
Recipe Name	
Cookbook	Page
Recipe Name	
Cookbook	Page
Recipe Name	
Cookbook	Page
Recipe Name	
Cookbook	Page
Recipe Name	
Cookbook	Page
Recipe Name	
Cookbook	Page
Recipe Name	
Cookbook	Page
Recipe Name	
Cookbook	Page

Favorite Recipe Index

Recipe Name	
Cookbook	Page
Recipe Name	
Cookbook	Page
Recipe Name	
Cookbook	Page
Recipe Name	
Cookbook	Page
Recipe Name	
Cookbook	Page
Recipe Name	
Cookbook	Page
Recipe Name	
Cookbook	Page
Recipe Name	
Cookbook	Page
Recipe Name	
Cookbook	Page
Recipe Name	
Cookbook	Page
Recipe Name	
Cookbook	Page

Favorite Recipe Index

Recipe Name	
Cookbook	Page
Recipe Name	
Cookbook	Page
Recipe Name	
Cookbook	Page
Recipe Name	
Cookbook	Page
Recipe Name	
Cookbook	Page
Recipe Name	
Cookbook	Page
Recipe Name	
Cookbook	Page
Recipe Name	
Cookbook	Page
Recipe Name	
Cookbook	Page
Recipe Name	
Cookbook	Page
Recipe Name	
Cookbook	Page

Favorite Recipe Index

Recipe Name	
Cookbook	Page
Recipe Name	
Cookbook	Page
Recipe Name	
Cookbook	Page
Recipe Name	
Cookbook	Page
Recipe Name	
Cookbook	Page
Recipe Name	
Cookbook	Page
Recipe Name	
Cookbook	Page
Recipe Name	
Cookbook	Page
Recipe Name	
Cookbook	Page
Recipe Name	
Cookbook	Page
Recipe Name	
Cookbook	Page

Favorite Recipes

Recipe Name	
From	Serves/ Yield

Favorite Recipes

Recipe Name	
From	Serves/ Yield

Favorite Recipes

Recipe Name	
From	Serves/ Yield

Favorite Recipes

Recipe Name	
From	Serves/ Yield

Favorite Recipes

Recipe Name	
From	Serves/ Yield

Favorite Recipes

Recipe Name	
From	Serves/ Yield

Favorite Recipes

Recipe Name	
From	Serves/ Yield

Favorite Recipes

Recipe Name	
From	Serves/ Yield

Favorite Recipes

Recipe Name	
From	Serves/ Yield

Favorite Recipes

Recipe Name	
From	Serves/ Yield

Favorite Recipes

Recipe Name	
From	Serves/ Yield

Favorite Recipes

Recipe Name	
From	Serves/ Yield

Favorite Recipes

Recipe Name	
From	Serves/ Yield

Favorite Recipes

Recipe Name	
From	Serves/ Yield

Favorite Recipes

Recipe Name	
From	Serves/ Yield

Favorite Recipes

Recipe Name	
From	Serves/ Yield

Favorite Recipes

Recipe Name	
From	Serves/ Yield

Favorite Recipes

Recipe Name	
From	Serves/ Yield

Vegetables
Rice–Pasta

Favorite Recipe Index

Recipe Name	
Cookbook	Page
Recipe Name	
Cookbook	Page
Recipe Name	
Cookbook	Page
Recipe Name	
Cookbook	Page
Recipe Name	
Cookbook	Page
Recipe Name	
Cookbook	Page
Recipe Name	
Cookbook	Page
Recipe Name	
Cookbook	Page
Recipe Name	
Cookbook	Page
Recipe Name	
Cookbook	Page
Recipe Name	
Cookbook	Page

Favorite Recipe Index

Recipe Name	
Cookbook	Page
Recipe Name	
Cookbook	Page
Recipe Name	
Cookbook	Page
Recipe Name	
Cookbook	Page
Recipe Name	
Cookbook	Page
Recipe Name	
Cookbook	Page
Recipe Name	
Cookbook	Page
Recipe Name	
Cookbook	Page
Recipe Name	
Cookbook	Page
Recipe Name	
Cookbook	Page
Recipe Name	
Cookbook	Page

Favorite Recipe Index

Recipe Name	
Cookbook	Page
Recipe Name	
Cookbook	Page
Recipe Name	
Cookbook	Page
Recipe Name	
Cookbook	Page
Recipe Name	
Cookbook	Page
Recipe Name	
Cookbook	Page
Recipe Name	
Cookbook	Page
Recipe Name	
Cookbook	Page
Recipe Name	
Cookbook	Page
Recipe Name	
Cookbook	Page
Recipe Name	
Cookbook	Page

Favorite Recipe Index

Recipe Name	
Cookbook	Page
Recipe Name	
Cookbook	Page
Recipe Name	
Cookbook	Page
Recipe Name	
Cookbook	Page
Recipe Name	
Cookbook	Page
Recipe Name	
Cookbook	Page
Recipe Name	
Cookbook	Page
Recipe Name	
Cookbook	Page
Recipe Name	
Cookbook	Page
Recipe Name	
Cookbook	Page
Recipe Name	
Cookbook	Page

Favorite Recipes

Recipe Name	
From	Serves/ Yield

Favorite Recipes

Recipe Name	
From	Serves/ Yield

Favorite Recipes

Recipe Name	
From	Serves/ Yield

Favorite Recipes

Recipe Name	
From	Serves/ Yield

Favorite Recipes

Recipe Name	
From	Serves/ Yield

Favorite Recipes

Recipe Name

From

Serves/
Yield

Favorite Recipes

Recipe Name

From

Serves/
Yield

Favorite Recipes

Recipe Name	
From	Serves/ Yield

Favorite Recipes

Recipe Name

From

Serves/
Yield

Favorite Recipes

Recipe Name	
From	Serves/ Yield

Favorite Recipes

Recipe Name

From

Serves/
Yield

Favorite Recipes

Recipe Name	
From	Serves/ Yield

Favorite Recipes

Recipe Name	
From	Serves/ Yield

Favorite Recipes

Recipe Name	
From	Serves/ Yield

Favorite Recipes

Recipe Name	
From	Serves/ Yield

Favorite Recipes

Recipe Name	
From	Serves/ Yield

Favorite Recipes

Recipe Name	
From	Serves/ Yield

Favorite Recipes

Recipe Name	
From	Serves/ Yield

Favorite Recipes

Recipe Name	
From	Serves/ Yield

Favorite Recipes

Recipe Name	
From	Serves/ Yield

Entrees

Favorite Recipe Index

* Recipe Name	Savory Crust Chicken Bake (Turkey) / stuffing taste to crust great leftover turkey	
Cookbook	Pillsbury 21st Bake-Off	Page 52
Recipe Name	Quick Crescent Taco Pie - good spicy & filling	
Cookbook	Pillsbury 21st Bake-Off	Page 65
Recipe Name		
Cookbook		Page
Recipe Name		
Cookbook		Page
Recipe Name		
Cookbook		Page
Recipe Name		
Cookbook		Page
Recipe Name		
Cookbook		Page
Recipe Name		
Cookbook		Page
Recipe Name		
Cookbook		Page
Recipe Name		
Cookbook		Page
Recipe Name		
Cookbook		Page

Favorite Recipe Index

Recipe Name	
Cookbook	Page
Recipe Name	
Cookbook	Page
Recipe Name	
Cookbook	Page
Recipe Name	
Cookbook	Page
Recipe Name	
Cookbook	Page
Recipe Name	
Cookbook	Page
Recipe Name	
Cookbook	Page
Recipe Name	
Cookbook	Page
Recipe Name	
Cookbook	Page
Recipe Name	
Cookbook	Page

Favorite Recipe Index

Recipe Name	
Cookbook	Page
Recipe Name	
Cookbook	Page
Recipe Name	
Cookbook	Page
Recipe Name	
Cookbook	Page
Recipe Name	
Cookbook	Page
Recipe Name	
Cookbook	Page
Recipe Name	
Cookbook	Page
Recipe Name	
Cookbook	Page
Recipe Name	
Cookbook	Page
Recipe Name	
Cookbook	Page
Recipe Name	
Cookbook	Page

Favorite Recipe Index

Recipe Name	
Cookbook	Page
Recipe Name	
Cookbook	Page
Recipe Name	
Cookbook	Page
Recipe Name	
Cookbook	Page
Recipe Name	
Cookbook	Page
Recipe Name	
Cookbook	Page
Recipe Name	
Cookbook	Page
Recipe Name	
Cookbook	Page
Recipe Name	
Cookbook	Page
Recipe Name	
Cookbook	Page
Recipe Name	
Cookbook	Page

Favorite Recipes

Recipe Name	
From	Serves/ Yield

Favorite Recipes

Recipe Name	
From	Serves/ Yield

Favorite Recipes

Recipe Name	
From	Serves/ Yield

Favorite Recipes

Recipe Name	
From	Serves/ Yield

Favorite Recipes

Recipe Name	
From	Serves/ Yield

Favorite Recipes

Recipe Name	
From	Serves/ Yield

Favorite Recipes

Recipe Name	
From	Serves/ Yield

Favorite Recipes

Recipe Name	
From	Serves/ Yield

Favorite Recipes

Recipe Name	
From	Serves/ Yield

Favorite Recipes

Recipe Name	
From	Serves/ Yield

Favorite Recipes

Recipe Name	
From	Serves/ Yield

Favorite Recipes

Recipe Name

From

Serves/
Yield

Favorite Recipes

Recipe Name

From

Serves/
Yield

Favorite Recipes

Recipe Name	
From	Serves/ Yield

Favorite Recipes

Recipe Name

From

Serves/
Yield

Favorite Recipes

Recipe Name	
From	Serves/ Yield

Favorite Recipes

Recipe Name

From

Serves/
Yield

Favorite Recipes

Recipe Name	
From	Serves/ Yield

Favorite Recipes

Recipe Name

From

Serves/
Yield

Favorite Recipes

Recipe Name

From

Serves/
Yield

Desserts

Favorite Recipe Index

Recipe Name	Chocolate Chip Cookies	
Cookbook	Silver Palate Cookbook	Page 262
Recipe Name	Chocolate Pixies	
Cookbook	Pillsbury Bake Off Cookies CB	Page 99
Recipe Name	Almond Buttercups	
Cookbook	Pillsbury Bake Off Cookies CB	Page 111
Recipe Name		
Cookbook		Page
Recipe Name		
Cookbook		Page
Recipe Name		
Cookbook		Page
Recipe Name		
Cookbook		Page
Recipe Name		
Cookbook		Page
Recipe Name		
Cookbook		Page
Recipe Name		
Cookbook		Page
Recipe Name		
Cookbook		Page

Favorite Recipe Index

Recipe Name	
Cookbook	Page
Recipe Name	
Cookbook	Page
Recipe Name	
Cookbook	Page
Recipe Name	
Cookbook	Page
Recipe Name	
Cookbook	Page
Recipe Name	
Cookbook	Page
Recipe Name	
Cookbook	Page
Recipe Name	
Cookbook	Page
Recipe Name	
Cookbook	Page
Recipe Name	
Cookbook	Page

Favorite Recipe Index

Recipe Name	
Cookbook	Page
Recipe Name	
Cookbook	Page
Recipe Name	
Cookbook	Page
Recipe Name	
Cookbook	Page
Recipe Name	
Cookbook	Page
Recipe Name	
Cookbook	Page
Recipe Name	
Cookbook	Page
Recipe Name	
Cookbook	Page
Recipe Name	
Cookbook	Page
Recipe Name	
Cookbook	Page
Recipe Name	
Cookbook	Page

Favorite Recipe Index

Recipe Name	
Cookbook	Page
Recipe Name	
Cookbook	Page
Recipe Name	
Cookbook	Page
Recipe Name	
Cookbook	Page
Recipe Name	
Cookbook	Page
Recipe Name	
Cookbook	Page
Recipe Name	
Cookbook	Page
Recipe Name	
Cookbook	Page
Recipe Name	
Cookbook	Page
Recipe Name	
Cookbook	Page
Recipe Name	
Cookbook	Page

Favorite Recipes

Recipe Name	
From	Serves/ Yield

Favorite Recipes

Recipe Name	
From	Serves/ Yield

Favorite Recipes

Recipe Name	
From	Serves/ Yield

Favorite Recipes

Recipe Name	
From	Serves/ Yield

Favorite Recipes

Recipe Name

From

Serves/
Yield

Favorite Recipes

Recipe Name	
From	Serves/ Yield

Favorite Recipes

Recipe Name	
From	Serves/ Yield

Favorite Recipes

Recipe Name	
From	Serves/ Yield

Favorite Recipes

Recipe Name	
From	Serves/ Yield

Favorite Recipes

Recipe Name	
From	Serves/ Yield

Favorite Recipes

Recipe Name	
From	Serves/ Yield

Favorite Recipes

Recipe Name	
From	Serves/ Yield

Favorite Recipes

Recipe Name

From

Serves/
Yield

Favorite Recipes

Recipe Name	
From	Serves/ Yield

Favorite Recipes

Recipe Name

From

Serves/
Yield

Favorite Recipes

Recipe Name	
From	Serves/ Yield

Favorite Recipes

Recipe Name	
From	Serves/ Yield

Favorite Recipes

Recipe Name	
From	Serves/ Yield

Favorite Recipes

Recipe Name	
From	Serves/ Yield

Favorite Recipes

Recipe Name	
From	Serves/ Yield

Favorite Recipes

Recipe Name	
From	Serves/ Yield

Favorite Recipes

Recipe Name	
From	Serves/ Yield

Miscellaneous

Favorite Recipes

Recipe Name	
From	Serves/ Yield

Favorite Recipes

Recipe Name	
From	Serves/ Yield

Favorite Recipes

Recipe Name

From

Serves/
Yield

Favorite Recipes

Recipe Name	
From	Serves/ Yield

Favorite Recipes

Recipe Name	
From	Serves/ Yield

Favorite Recipes

Recipe Name	
From	Serves/ Yield

LB Publications
8338 San Leandro
Dallas, Texas 75218

Please send ________ copies of **FINDER'S KEEPERS.**

Price	$	9.95
Postage and handling	$	2.00
(Texas residents add tax)	$	.80
Total per book	$	______
Total amount enclosed	$	______

Make checks payable to **FINDER'S KEEPERS.**

Name ____________________

Address ____________________

City, State, Zip ____________________

LB Publications
8338 San Leandro
Dallas, Texas 75218

Please send ________ copies of **FINDER'S KEEPERS.**

Price	$	9.95
Postage and handling	$	2.00
(Texas residents add tax)	$	.80
Total per book	$	______
Total amount enclosed	$	______

Make checks payable to **FINDER'S KEEPERS.**

Name ____________________

Address ____________________

City, State, Zip ____________________

ORDER BOOKS HERE